Irresistible

Reclaiming the New
That Jesus Unleashed
for the World

STUDY GUIDE | SIX SESSIONS

ANDY STANLEY

ZONDERVAN

Irresistible Study Guide
Copyright © 2019 by Andy Stanley

Requests for information should be addressed to:
Zondervan, *3900 Sparks Dr. SE, Grand Rapids, Michigan 49546*

ISBN 978-0-310-10049-2 (softcover)

ISBN 978-0-310-10050-8 (ebook)

Art direction: Micah Kandros
Interior design: Kait Lamphere

First printing November 2018 / Printed in the United States of America

Contents

INTRODUCTION

Welcome to Andy Stanley's *Irresistible Video Study*. In the weeks to come, you'll be invited to take an honest look at the state of Christianity today, how it differs from the faith of those who were part of the first-century church, and what needs to happen to help us reclaim that same *irresistibility*. "Modern, mainstream Christianity is fatally flawed," Andy wrote. "These flaws make it fragile and indefensible in the public square."

That's the bad news.

The good news is this: We can reclaim what was once characteristic of those who were part of *The Way*. We can change course and head in a new direction. We can fulfill Jesus' dream for his church. And we can pursue these goals starting today.

As you prepare to begin your six-session experience, read through the following notes.

GATHERING A GROUP

This experience can be completed as a pair, a trio, or a group, but it is intended to be worked through in community, not in isolation. If you're not already in a group, find those friends, colleagues, or family members who might be interested in this subject matter, and extend an invitation to join in.

Prior to your first meeting to discuss Session 1, confirm the dates, times, and locations of all six sessions so that group members can block time for the gatherings and come prepared to engage.

NECESSARY SUPPLIES

Maximize your experience by ensuring that all group members have the following supplies prior to Session 1:

- This study guide

- Andy's book, *Irresistible: Reclaiming the New that Jesus Unleashed for the World* (Zondervan 2018)

- Bible, any translation (this guide uses the New International Version)

- Pen or pencil

FACILITATION TIPS

Help your group right from the start by designating a facilitator who will guide you through the content each time you gather. You might select one person to fill this role for all six sessions or several people who will rotate through the role. However you structure things, be sure to adhere to the following three guidelines for leading a group:

1. *Be prepared.* Prior to the group meeting, review the entire session, as well as that session's video segment. Make note of the highest-impact questions you'd like to ask in the event that discussion runs long and you don't have time to cover them all. Work through how you'd answer those questions in advance so you can prime the pump as the meeting unfolds. Plot the major sections of content (see "Session Flow" below) against the time you'll have so you're not caught off-guard in the moment.

2. *Be inclusive.* Work to include all personality types in your group. Gently draw out quiet members. Help redirect members who are prone to dominate the discussion. Work to create a safe space for each member to feel seen, valued, and encouraged.

3. *Be thoughtful.* Plan how you will segue from one section of content to the next. Will you offer a prayer before the video plays? Will you allow for moments of silence after the video and before the discussion begins for people to absorb what they've just heard? Think through how to best serve your group, and then resolve to do those things.

SESSION FLOW

The *Irresistible Video Study* comprises six sessions, each of which contains the following six parts:

1. Before You Begin :: A reminder of the chapters from *Irresistible* that will be covered

2. From *Irresistible* :: A centering quote from Andy's book, to be read prior to the video segment

3. Video Notes :: Space for group members to write thoughts and insights from the video segment

4. Discussion Questions :: Questions based on the video content

5. Wrap It Up :: A closing thought from *Irresistible*

6. Between Sessions :: Opportunities for group members to dive deeper into session content between group meetings

THE INVITATION

Near the end of *Irresistible*, Andy sums up the invitation that has been extended to every Christ follower:

In light of what's at stake and who is at stake, would you consider unhitching your teaching of what it means to follow Jesus from all things old covenant? Would you be willing to transfer your faith from a book to the events behind the book? Will you embrace this more endurable, defensible, liberating, culture-transforming version of our faith? That's a lot to ask. But while you're considering that, ask yourself this.

What is the faith of the next generation worth?

What is the faith of your children and grandchildren worth?

I say, everything. I say it's worth any change necessary to ensure the version of faith passed on to the next generation is the enduring version—the faith of our first-century fathers. The version that was harder than Roman steel and tougher than Roman nails. So will you consider retooling how you communicate in order to win some and save some? Will you adjust your language to avoid making it unnecessarily difficult for those who are turning toward God or turning back to God? Are you willing to embrace the realities of the world we live in and let go of cultural assumptions that characterized the world you grew up in?

Granted, these will be hard habits to break.

But break them we must.

The faith of the next generation may depend on it.

Ready to discover not only why this shift is necessary, but also how we can bring this vision to life?

Let's begin.

SESSION 1

Simply Resistible

Modern Bible readers see Jesus as an extension of the Jewish Scriptures, our Old Testament. Jewish leaders in Jesus' day didn't see him as an extension or fulfillment of anything. . . . From their vantage point, Jesus was introducing something new. On this, they were correct.

Andy Stanley

BEFORE YOU BEGIN

A quick reading reminder before you dive in:

Session 1 covers material from the Introduction to Section 1 and the first five chapters in *Irresistible*:

- Introduction to Section 1: Simply Resistible

- Chapter 1 :: The New Standard American Version

- Chapter 2 :: Going Global

- Chapter 3 :: Temple Tantrum

- Chapter 4 :: Splittin' Up

- Chapter 5 :: Recentering the Universe

FROM *IRRESISTIBLE* . . .

Before playing this session's video, have a group member read the following:

The decline of Christianity in America, the popularity of the New Atheists, and the meteoric rise of the *nones* underscore something that's been true for generations but didn't matter much until now. Modern, mainstream Christianity is fatally flawed. These flaws make it fragile and indefensible in the public square. . . .

The way forward is not complicated, though some will find it controversial. It's not original with me. It's hidden in plain sight in the Gospels and the epistles of Paul. We know it *works* because it already *worked*. Once upon a time, members of a Jewish cult called *The Way*, against all odds, captured the attention and, ultimately, the dedication of the pagan world, both inside and outside the Roman Empire. So perhaps we need to hit pause on much of what we're doing today—which isn't working all that well anyway—and take notes from the men and women credited with turning the world upside down.

VIDEO NOTES

As you watch Session 1 of the video, feel free to take notes in the space below.

Why doesn't everyone in America go to church?

What first-century Christians knew that we don't

Jesus as greater than the temple

"But all the cool kids have kings . . ."

Purpose of the prophets

Silence, and then the Messiah

DISCUSSION QUESTIONS

Cover as many of the following questions as time and group interest permit.

1. What comment of Andy's stood out to you most? What emotion did it provoke? Share your thoughts with your group.

2. If the young woman in the story Andy told asked *you* why everyone in America doesn't go to church, what would you have said?

3. The young woman's question bothered Andy. Would such a question (and the implications of that question) bother you? Why or why not?

4. Andy made the assertion that the church is indeed "so resistible" today. What do you think he means? Do you see evidence to back up such a claim?

5. Have you or someone you know struggled with some of the issues cited in the video segment (noted below) regarding why people have abandoned the faith?

   ☐ Disparity between the seemingly violent and capricious God of the Old Testament and the gentle, grace-filled Jesus, who is presented in the New Testament

   ☐ Contradictions regarding biblical "facts"

   ☐ The prevalence of suffering in the world

   ☐ Confusion regarding the age of the earth, the veracity of the great flood, etc.

   ☐ Scientific hang-ups such as climate change, natural selection, and so forth

This study's subtitle refers to *reclaiming* something we as believers once had. What do you think that thing was that kept the early church from being derailed by issues such as these?

6. In the video segment, Andy reviewed ten key events during God's covenantal commitment to Abraham. Have members look up the verse(s) and note the key points in the spaces below.

   Genesis 17:15–19

   Exodus 1:1–14

Joshua 10:1–13

1 Samuel 9:15–10:1

1 Samuel 16:1–13

2 Samuel 7:1–29

1 Kings 10:26–11:6

Ezra 6:1–12

2 Kings 17:7–17

Malachi 3:1–18

7. What do you take away from this sweep through ancient history?

8. What misunderstandings could unfold for someone who might be interested in following Jesus but who is stymied by these Old Testament events?

FROM *IRRESISTIBLE*:

The distinguishing characteristic of the Jewish temple was not something it included that the competition lacked. Quite the opposite. The differentiating characteristic of the Jewish temple was something it lacked that everybody else had.

An image.

The holy of holies was like a beautiful, ornately designed frame without a picture. This was why Israel didn't need a temple to begin with. The distinguishing characteristic of Judaism was not the design of their temple. It was the lack of an image representing their God. Images were strictly forbidden in Judaism. As we discovered earlier, this particular prohibition was one of the Big Ten.

The notion of worshiping an image or idol is so foreign to us that an empty idol chamber doesn't strike us as odd. But in ancient times, the very opposite was true.

WRAP IT UP

Remind the group of the "Between Sessions" material that follows, offer a closing thought or prayer based on the quote below, and then dismiss Session 1.

While it could be argued God was silent in the years of Israel's occupation and oppression, he certainly wasn't still.
—*Andy Stanley*

Session 1

BETWEEN SESSIONS

Following each session, you're invited to go a little deeper with the content your group discussed. In each of these "Between Sessions" segments, you'll find an extended excerpt from Andy's book followed by questions for reflection.

THE EXCERPT

When you read Jesus' description of what would transpire within view of where he was seated, it's easy to imagine the pain in his voice. It was as if he could see the carnage, hear the screams, and feel the panic of mothers clinging to their children.

These were his people. This was his nation. The nation God had raised up from one man for one purpose—to bless the world. But that chapter was drawing to a close. The temple era was coming to an end. God's covenant with the nation had served its purpose. It was no longer needed.

Why?

Because something *greater* than the temple had come.

Something that would make the temple and everything associated with it obsolete. Something new. Something better. Something for the whole world. Ancient Israel was a means to an end.

The end had come.

The new was just beginning.

GIVE IT SOME THOUGHT

➡ Why would God establish a covenant that ultimately would not be needed? Why go through the trouble of allowing the Old Testament twists and turns when "something better" would eventually straighten things out?

➡ Even without them recognizing it, why might God's nation of Israel have craved something *new*?

In *Irresistible*, Andy notes a few of the old-way remnants that deeply troubled Jesus as he began his ministry here on earth. He wrote:

By the time Jesus reached adulthood, the Jewish temple system was completely corrupt. He thought so anyway. While we're introduced to a smattering of sincere priests, lawyers, and Pharisees in the Gospels, they are the exception. Jesus' trial alone is enough to remove any doubt about the state of the state.

The widespread corruption in the religious community is not simply inferred and illustrated in the Gospels. Jesus addressed it directly. In Matthew's Gospel, we find Jesus' description of the men in charge. Here's a sampling:

- Everything they do is done for people to see.

- They love the place of honor at banquets.

- They love their titles.

- They love to be greeted with respect in the marketplaces.

- They neglect justice, mercy, and faithfulness.

- They are hypocrites.

- They are full of greed and self-indulgence.

- On the outside they appear righteous, but on the inside they are full of wickedness.

➡ Choose one item from the list above. How might an "old covenant" mindset fuel that manifestation?

➡ When have you seen this type of behavior still today?

REMINDER: To prepare for Session 2, be sure to read the Introduction to Section 2 and Chapters 6–7 in *Irresistible*.

SESSION 2

Brand-New Agreement

God had an agenda. His agenda had implications for all nations, not *a* nation. And it had implications for you . . . and for the you sitting next to you.

Andy Stanley

BEFORE YOU BEGIN

A quick reminder before you dive in:

Session 2 covers material from the Introduction to Section 2 and two chapters in *Irresistible*:

- Introduction to Section 2: All Things New

- Chapter 6 :: Brand-New Movement

- Chapter 7 :: Brand-New Agreement

FROM *IRRESISTIBLE* . . .

Before playing this session's video, have a group member read the following:

On the evening prior to his crucifixion, which nobody in the room saw coming, Jesus met with the Twelve for the Passover meal. Passover was one of the most, if not *the* most, important celebrations for ancient Jews. . . . Jesus used his final Passover meal to announce the end of Passover as they knew it and to signal the inauguration of a new covenant. Not a new covenant between God and an individual, as was the case with Abraham. Not a covenant between God and a particular nation, as was the case with Israel. This was the big one.

The final one.

The everlasting one.

This was a covenant between God and the human race. Every nation for every generation. The inauguration of a new covenant signaled the *fulfillment* of God's promise to Abraham. Finally, something for everybody. With the inauguration of the new covenant, every nation would be blessed.

VIDEO NOTES

As you watch Session 2 of the video, feel free to take notes in the space below.

God's agenda for *a* nation . . . God's agenda for *all* nations

The arrival of something "brand-new"

The most offensive statement ever

On smuggling the old into the new

The *Five Solas*

Mix-and-match in the modern church

DISCUSSION QUESTIONS

Cover as many of the following questions as time and group interest permit.

1. What comment of Andy's provoked you most? What got your attention? What made you feel angry/curious/understood/protective/annoyed?

2. Early in the video segment, Andy said that despite his strong opinions on how we perceive the Old Testament, he's not "discounting the importance of the Jewish Scripture." Andy is actually trumpeting the perspective Jesus himself holds. Before looking up the verses in question #3, what do you think was "Jesus' perspective" on the Old Testament/old covenant/Hebrew Bible/Law?

3. Have each member (or pair of members) look up one of the passages below and report back what it says to the full group.

Jeremiah 31:31–34

Hebrews 8:4–13

Hebrews 13:9–16, 20–21

4. What is the common denominator in the passages from question #3? What word do all these verses use to describe the covenant Jesus came to usher in?

5. The idea of something *new* can elicit strong emotions in a person. Take a moment to jot down the primary emotion you feel as you read each phrase below. Once everyone is done, share a few examples with your group of why you wrote down the emotions you did.

New season: _____

New job: _____

New friend: _____

New car: _____

New habit: _____

New information: _____

New thinking: _____

New chapter: _____

New beginning: _____

New attitude: _____

New home: _____

New neighbor: _____

New challenge: _____

New experience: _____

New wardrobe: _____

New perspective: _____

New goal: _____

New things don't generally bother us, Andy noted in the video, until we realize "new" means letting go of "old." Give an example from the list above of a new thing not exactly being a welcomed change because it would mean letting go of the old. Share your thoughts with your group.

6. When Jesus arrived on the scene, the Jewish people who encountered him had a definite emotional response. They would have filled in the blank this way:

New covenant: *outrage!* _____

No kidding: outrage. Why? Because what Jesus was saying was *outrageous*. Case in point: what we refer to as "the Last Supper" was Jesus' final meal with his disciples before he would be arrested, abused, and killed.

What does Exodus 12 say about the origins of the annual Jewish Passover celebration (also known as the Festival of Unleavened Bread)? Specifically . . .

- Was this a big deal?

- Did God provide lots of instructions or just a few?

- Were Passover preparations extensive and possibly exhausting, or minimal and pretty quick?

- Were the ramifications of not following Passover protocol significant or inconsequential? In other words, how much was on the line?

The "outrageous" thing that Jesus said? From Luke 22:

> When the hour came, Jesus and his apostles reclined at the table. And he said to them, "I have eagerly desired to eat this Passover with you before I suffer. For I tell you, I will not eat it again until it finds fulfillment in the kingdom of God."
>
> After taking the cup, he gave thanks and said, "Take this and divide it among you. For I tell you I will not drink again from the fruit of the vine until the kingdom of God comes."
>
> And he took bread, gave thanks and broke it, and gave it to them, saying, "This is my body given for you; do this in remembrance of me," (vv. 14–19).

It's that last bit that stirred the men up: "Do this in remembrance of me."

From *Irresistible*:

> Jesus reframed and reinterpreted a meal pointing back to perhaps the most pivotal moment in Israel's history. Put yourself in the disciples' sandals and imagine how ridiculous, how blasphemous, this must have sounded. We don't mess with Christmas or Easter, and Jesus didn't have any business messing with Passover.

> At that dinner with his disciples, Jesus would give the reason for his seemingly outrageous remark: "In the same way, after the supper he [Jesus] took the cup, saying, 'This cup is the *new covenant* in my blood, which is poured out for you.'"

In essence, Jesus was saying, "I've come to bring something *new*." How do you feel about that?

7. Toward the end of the video segment, Andy addressed what he calls "mix-and-match theology." Which of the following examples best reflects your observations of contemporary Christianity? Which are the most detrimental to the cause of Christ, and why?

- Christians are moving to post the Ten Commandments in classrooms and courtrooms.

- Children are handed copies of the old covenant bound with the new, with no explanation as to the difference between the two.

- Some churches have priests.

- Christians refer to their pastors as "anointed."

- Some Christian leaders warn of God's impending judgment.

- Some Christians believe God is "judging the nations."

- Christian parents are kicking out their son or daughter for being gay or pregnant.

- Christian leaders declare a tsunami of God's judgment on Muslim regions of the world.

- Christians judge non-Christians for their non-Christian behavior.

- Pastors broad-brush scriptural references by saying, "The Bible says . . ."

- Christians glean dating and marital advice from King Solomon (the biblical book "The Song of Songs"), who had more than 700 wives and an additional 300 concubines.

What additional examples of mix-and-match theology can your group come up with? Brainstorm for a few moments, logging your collective thoughts in the space below.

WRAP IT UP

Remind participants of the "Between Sessions" material that follows, offer a closing thought or prayer based on the quote below, and then dismiss Session 2.

> As long as we cling to the *old* Jesus came
> to replace, we will never fully appreciate, experience,
> or even recognize the *new* he came to put in place.
> **—Andy Stanley**

Session 2

BETWEEN SESSIONS

In each of these "Between Sessions" segments, you'll find an extended excerpt from Andy's book followed by questions for reflection.

THE EXCERPT

Now, to be clear, none of this [our propensity to mix and match old covenant specifics with new covenant living] is a big deal as long as we are content creating closed church cultures designed by and for church people. For those churches, the blending of old with new simply creates unique religious expressions, theological differentiators, and a broad range of song lyrics. No harm done.

But . . .

But if you . . . if I . . . if we . . . desire to participate in the *ekklesia* of Jesus, there is no room for rebranded, repurposed, and retrofitted old. What some may be inclined to adopt as a *distinctive*, we must reject as *error*. The reformers refused to accept salvation via penance as a theological distinctive. They held it up against the new covenant and put a label on it. Error.

What's at stake goes beyond theological correctness. This is about the Great Commission. It's about evangelism. This is about the *ekklesia* of Jesus functioning as salt and unfiltered light. This is about ensuring that the life-changing *new* Jesus unleashed in the world doesn't get retrofitted with something old. Retro is fine for your middle-school daughter's bedroom. It's not fine for the church. To paraphrase James, the brother of Jesus, this is about not making it unnecessarily difficult for those who are turning to God. To paraphrase the apostle Paul, this is about winning some and saving some.

GIVE IT SOME THOUGHT

➡ In the passage above, how does Andy describe the person/people/ organization for whom the tendency to hold to a mix-and-match theology is no big deal?

➡ How would you describe what Andy refers to as "closed church cultures designed by and for church people"?

➡ When have you been part of a closed religious culture, and what was your experience like? What might motivate people to value such a culture?

➡ The Great Commission was instruction that Jesus offered to his disciples—both then and now—before he concluded his earthly ministry and returned to his Father's side in heaven. What observations do you make regarding Jesus' words below? Note them in the space that follows.

Then the eleven disciples went to Galilee, to the mountain where Jesus had told them to go. When they saw him, they worshiped him; but some doubted. Then Jesus came to them and said, "All authority in heaven and on earth has been given to me. Therefore go and make disciples of all nations, baptizing them in the name of the Father and of the Son and of the Holy Spirit, and teaching them to obey everything I have commanded you. And surely I am with you always, to the very end of the age."

—Matthew 28:16–20

➡ How might "closed church cultures" stand in direct opposition both to the intent and to the content of the Great Commission?

➡ What characteristics do you think might mark an "open" church culture?

➡ Would you say you're more "closed" or more "open" to those living far from God? What attitudes, assumptions, or experiences might be shaping your response?

➡ In what ways are you prone to making it difficult for people to encounter Christ? Do you tend to expect "Christian" behavior even from non-Christians? Do you hold to a list of spoken or unspoken rules? Is there some sort of "bar" in your mind that people must clear before they are welcomed into your sphere? Something else? Note your thoughts below.

REMINDER: To prepare for Session 3, be sure to read Chapters 8–13 in *Irresistible*.

The Bible According To Jesus

Old covenant leftovers explain why religious leaders feel it's their responsibility to rail against the evils in society like an Old Testament prophet. . . . Bad church experiences are almost always related to old covenant remnants.

Andy Stanley

BEFORE YOU BEGIN

A quick reading reminder before you dive in:

Session 3 covers material from six chapters in *Irresistible*:

- Chapter 8 :: Your First Look at the Good Book

- Chapter 9 :: The Bible According to Jesus

- Chapter 10 :: Homebodies

- Chapter 11 :: The Apoplectic Apostle

- Chapter 12 :: Obsolete-r Than Ever

- Chapter 13 :: Our Old Friend

FROM *IRRESISTIBLE* . . .

Before playing this session's video, have a group member read the following:

If you grew up attending a conservative Bible-believing church, the *entire* Bible was authoritative, not just the New Testament—all sixty-six books. Consequently, from day one, many of us were unintentionally encouraged to mix, match, and blend Old Testament concepts and values with New. It's unlikely anyone explained to you that the Bible is organized around several covenants or contracts between God and a variety of people and people groups. Odds are, nobody explained why the Old Testament was called old and the New, new. The entire book seemed old, didn't it?

What you *were* told, or figured out on your own, was that the New Testament was about Jesus. Mostly, anyway. And thus your relationship with the Bible began.

VIDEO NOTES

As you watch Session 3 of the video, feel free to take notes in the space below.

Your first Bible

Where mixing and matching has left us

Was the old covenant flawed?

Why the Old Testament is called "old"

The dangers of presenting an "all skate"

Jesus' greater-than-Moses answers to common dilemmas

DISCUSSION QUESTIONS

Cover as many of the following questions as time and group interest permit.

1. What struck you most from this week's video segment, and why?

2. If you own a copy of the Bible, how did you come to own it? Who gave it to you, and what explanation for it did you receive? Given what you know today, was the information helpful or not, and why?

3. What do you make of Andy's assertion, "Bad church experiences are almost always related to old covenant remnants," and, "Most bad church experiences are the result of somebody prioritizing a *view* over a *you*, something Jesus never did and instructed us not to do either"? Do any "bad church experiences" come to mind?

4. In this week's reading, Andy cited three examples of imports from the Old Testament that do us no favors today: self-righteousness, legalism, and the prosperity gospel.

   a. How do any of these "imports" relate to the requirements of the old covenant?

   b. Have you ever seen these specific deviations from grace crop up in your own life?

5. In *Irresistible*, Andy stated the "issue" we face with respect to how to regard the Old Testament, writing:

> The justifications Christians have used since the fourth century to mistreat people find their roots in old covenant practices and values. As I mentioned in the Introduction, imagine trying to leverage the Sermon on the Mount to start an inquisition, launch a crusade, or incite a pogrom against Jews. But reach back into the old covenant, and there's plenty to work with.

> But to be clear, I'm not saying there is plenty to work with because God's covenant with Israel was flawed. Just the opposite. When understood in its ancient context, it was brilliant!

For starters, what do you think would happen if someone tried to instigate discriminatory or hateful activity based on the contents of the Sermon on the Mount?

Which segments from that sermon (below) might they use?

Blessed are the poor in spirit,
    for theirs is the kingdom of heaven.
Blessed are those who mourn,
    for they will be comforted.
Blessed are the meek,
    for they will inherit the earth.
Blessed are those who hunger and thirst for righteousness,
    for they will be filled.
Blessed are the merciful,
    for they will be shown mercy.
Blessed are the pure in heart,
    for they will see God.
Blessed are the peacemakers,
    for they will be called children of God.
Blessed are those who are persecuted because of righteousness,
    for theirs is the kingdom of heaven.

Blessed are you when people insult you, persecute you and falsely say all kinds of evil against you because of me. Rejoice and be glad, because great is your reward in heaven, for in the same way they persecuted the prophets who were before you. (Matthew 5:3–12)

On the flip side, what hopes, dreams, resolutions, convictions, confirmations, and emotions rise to the surface of your mind and heart as you read Jesus' words?

6. As a group, discuss your thoughts on the prompts below, expounding on what you think about this statement from Andy in *Irresistible*: "The old covenant, God's covenant with Israel, was a package deal. It was all or nothing. The fact that someone chose to publish the old covenant with the new covenant in a genuine leather binding doesn't mean we should treat them or apply them the same way. The Bible is all God's Word . . . to *somebody*. But it's not all God's word to *everybody*."

- Who wrote the Bible?

- Who was the Bible written to?

- What was the purpose for the Bible being written?

- Why has the Bible lasted all these years?

- Is the Bible true?

- Is the writing inspired?

- Is it consistent?

- Is it reliable?

- Is it useful for daily life?

7. One of the Bible's greatest injunctions to Christ followers is the Great Commission, which we looked at last time. It says this:

> Then the eleven disciples went to Galilee, to the mountain where Jesus had told them to go. When they saw him, they worshiped him; but some doubted. Then Jesus came to them and said, "All authority in heaven and on earth has been given to me. Therefore go and make disciples of all nations, baptizing them in the name of the Father and of the Son and of the Holy Spirit, and teaching them to obey everything I have commanded you. And surely I am with you always, to the very end of the age."
>
> —Matthew 28:16–20

Admittedly, there are things Jesus has commanded us that people who long to come into his kingdom must obey. What do you think that list of commands includes?

WRAP IT UP

Remind participants of the "Between Sessions" material that follows, offer a closing thought or prayer based on the quote below, and then dismiss Session 3.

**Most of what makes us resistible are things
we should have been resisting all along.
—Andy Stanley**

Session 3

BETWEEN SESSIONS

In each of these "Between Sessions" segments, you'll find an extended excerpt from Andy's book followed by brief exercises for both contemplation and action.

THE EXCERPT

As the hinge between the old and new covenants, Jesus was in the unenviable position of playing by an old set of rules while laying the groundwork for what was to come. He showed respect and deference to the old but was uncomfortably clear that something new was on the horizon. . . .

One example of this foreshadowing is found in his most famous sermon. . . .

In Matthew's account, after getting everybody's attention with a unique take on how to be happy, Jesus put a new spin on several familiar commandments and traditions, commandments and traditions his audience had been taught since childhood.

You have heard that . . .

As in: *Your entire life the people you trust and respect have told you . . .*

> You have heard that it was said, "Eye for eye, and tooth for tooth."

Yes, they had. The Jewish Scriptures stated:

> Show no pity: life for life, eye for eye, tooth for tooth, hand for hand, foot for foot.

Instead of explaining what that bit of Scripture meant, Jesus surprised everyone with this:

> But . . .

If he had paused after "But . . ." they would have thought, *But? Jesus, you don't respond to Moses with but unless it's, "But of course." You can't but something handed down by Moses!*

But he did.

Because Jesus was greater than Moses. Greater than the temple. Greater than the law. So he butted his way through.

> But I tell you do not resist an evil person. If anyone slaps you on the right cheek, turn to them the other cheek also. And if anyone wants to sue you and take your shirt, hand over your coat as well. If anyone forces you to go one mile, go with them two miles.

We can't begin to imagine how ridiculous this sounded to first-century Jews struggling to survive under the hobnailed sandals of Rome. But more to the point of our discussion, we can't begin to imagine how *unbiblical* this sounded to first-century Jews whose entire Scriptures were built on an ethic to the contrary.

You're familiar enough with Old Testament stories to know Israel never, ever, turned the other cheek. Joshua, the messiah figure for first-century Jews, was certainly not a cheek turner. He was a warrior. David, in whose line the Messiah was to come, had so much blood on his hands God wouldn't let him build the temple. Jesus wasn't simply contradicting their Scriptures. His teaching stood in stark contrast to their entire story!

GIVE IT SOME THOUGHT

In this session, we looked at the difference between conditional and unconditional covenants, the designations of which you probably never heard before and never will hear again. But for the purpose of this section, here they are:

- *Bilateral Suzerain Treaty*: a covenant between non-equals; a conditional covenant that said, "As long as you—whether a person, a group, a nation—keep your end of the bargain, I'll keep mine."

- *Promissory Covenant*: a unilateral, unconditional covenant that said, "I, one party, pledge to you, the other party, to take full responsibility for fulfilling this agreement."

➡ Given the Israelites' inability to keep the terms of the Law throughout the Old Testament, why do you suppose it was necessary for God to enact a totally different kind of covenant between humankind and his Son?

➡ If in the "promissory covenant" Jesus takes full responsibility for fulfilling the entire agreement—both God's part and also ours—then why do you think we're told in the Great Commission to obey certain commands? Doesn't the new covenant—of acceptance and grace and love—free us from such restrictions and duties?

In this session's video segment, Andy described in gruesome detail the lengths Jesus went to so that this covenant with his Father could be fulfilled. He said: "On that very night [Passover], he [Jesus] would surrender his own body to be flayed to the bone by a Roman cat-of-nine-tails. Minutes later, he would be forced to shoulder a wooden beam weighing upwards of a hundred pounds. Then his hands and feet would literally be torn in two by his own weight as he hung and bled to death on a Roman cross: "This cup is the new covenant in my blood which is poured out for you." It was Jesus' way of saying to the world: "This is on me, for you!"

Look up the following six verses. In the space below each, log what the passage teaches about who is responsible for "living up to" the demands inherent in Jesus' new covenant of love and grace.

Ephesians 6:10

Philippians 4:13

2 Timothy 1:7

Matthew 19:26

Ephesians 1:19–20

2 Timothy 2:1

➡ Based on the above Scriptures, how is it possible for believers to uphold the counsel from the Sermon on the Mount—loving one's enemies, going the extra mile, and so forth?

➡ What might a person's unwillingness or inability to engage in such practices reveal about whether they have truly embraced Christ's unconditional love for us?

REMINDER: To prepare for Session 4, be sure to read the Introduction to Section 3 and Chapter 14 in *Irresistible.*

The Irresistible Ethic

Faith disconnected from love leads to legalism, an eye-to-the-sky, vertical morality that doesn't concern itself with loving others.

Andy Stanley

BEFORE YOU BEGIN

A quick reminder before you dive in:

Session 4 covers material from the Introduction to Section 3 and Chapter 14.

- Introduction to Section 3: A New Ethic

- Chapter 14 :: Trending Horizontal

FROM *IRRESISTIBLE* . . .

Before playing this session's video, have a group member read the following:

In the stream of Christianity I grew up in, sin avoidance was pretty much our guiding light. As I understood it, as long as I wasn't breaking a God rule, I was good with God and God was good with me. It was well with my soul. God was free to hear and, hopefully, answer my prayers. The whole thing was vertical. I was far more concerned about how my behavior affected my standing with God than I was about how my behavior affected anybody else. After all, the Bible says pleasing God is more important than pleasing people. Which led me to conclude that if I sinned against *you*, and asked God to forgive *me*, everything would be good between God and me even if things weren't good between you and me. I could have a clear conscience with God while continuing to avoid you in the grocery store. . . .

Of course, there's a bit of hypocrisy woven into all this. My primary concern was not how my sin affected God. My primary concern was me!

VIDEO NOTES

As you watch Session 4 of the video, feel free to take notes in the space below.

"Is _____ a sin?"

How high can we get?

When horizontal takes precedence over vertical

To love the Lord your God with all your heart, soul, strength, and mind

To love my neighbor as myself

Neighbor-love as evidence of God-love

DISCUSSION QUESTIONS

Cover as many of the following questions as time and group interest permit.

1. What did you think of this session's video segment? What struck you as most impactful? Who *is* your neighbor, anyway?

2. What do you make of the "vertical morality" concept Andy introduced? How do *you* complete the question, "Is _____ a sin?"

Have you ever wondered how your behavior sits with God? Who planted that thought in your mind?

3. How does Andy's explanation mesh with your own understanding of our tendency toward "vertical morality" being a remnant of God's *intentionally vertical* covenant with the nation of Israel? He said: "He [God] was creating a nation from scratch. He needed their undivided attention. The preamble to the Sinai covenant underscores that. . . . In a nutshell, God's message to Israel was: *'Keep your eyes on me and my commandments or else!'* Doesn't get more vertical than that."

4. If you were to take to the streets, asking strangers how they would answer the question, "What do you think it means to love God with all your heart, soul, mind, and strength?" what types of answers do you think you'd receive? Check all that apply and then fill in your own additions below.

☐ "Read my Bible."

☐ "Be a good person."

☐ "Go to church."

☐ "Don't sin."

☐ "Pray."

☐ "Don't have sex before marriage."

☐ "Don't drink. Don't do drugs."

☐ "Don't lie or cheat or steal."

☐ "Give money to the church."

☐ "Volunteer."

☐ "That whole 'do unto others' thing"

☐ _____

☐ _____

Considering your responses, what percentage of the expected answers are rooted in old covenant thinking, old covenant relating to God? Why is this?

5. In this week's video segment, Andy alludes both to "vertical morality"—
   how we relate directly to God—and to "horizontal morality"—how
   we relate to people we come across. Think back on your own spiritual
   journey. Which statement below is truer to your experience? Select one,
   and then talk with your group about why you think this is so.

   ☐ I feel better about my relationship with God when I am
   keeping his commands and generally being a "good person."

   ☐ I feel better about my relationship with God when I am
   helping others gain access to the resources they need, solve
   problems, and generally sort out life.

6. Take a few minutes to scan the following passages of Scripture. What is
   the common denominator you see in each of them? (Note it in the space
   that follows.)

Hebrews 6:10

God is not unjust; he will not forget your work and the love you have
shown him as you have helped his people and continue to help them.

Galatians 5:13

You, my brothers and sisters, were called to be free. But do not use
your freedom to indulge the flesh; rather, serve one another humbly
in love.

Romans 7:6

But now, by dying to what once bound us, we have been released from the law so that we serve in the new way of the Spirit, and not in the old way of the written code.

John 12:26

Whoever serves me must follow me; and where I am, my servant also will be. My Father will honor the one who serves me.

1 Peter 4:10

Each of you should use whatever gift you have received to serve others, as faithful stewards of God's grace in its various forms.

Romans 12:9–13

Love must be sincere. Hate what is evil; cling to what is good. Be devoted to one another in love. Honor one another above yourselves. Never be lacking in zeal, but keep your spiritual fervor, serving the Lord. Be joyful in hope, patient in affliction, faithful in prayer. Share with the Lord's people who are in need. Practice hospitality.

7. When you feel unmotivated to show up for others, to extend a helping hand to others, to pray for or serve others, what's most often the reason? Select as many from the list below as are applicable, and discuss your thoughts with your group.

   ☐ "It will take too much time/money."

   ☐ "It will be too messy emotionally."

   ☐ "It's not my responsibility."

   ☐ "I'm afraid."

   ☐ "I don't want to be a bother."

   ☐ "I have enough problems of my own."

   ☐ Other: _____

8. Think of a need in someone else's life that you recently helped meet. What explanations/excuses did you have to overcome? How did things turn out?

In a similar vein, how might the experience inform your ability to keep showing up, to keep prizing kingdom-of-God living, to keep loving your neighbor?

WRAP IT UP

Remind participants of the "Between Sessions" material that follows, offer a closing thought or prayer based on the quote below, and then dismiss Session 4.

> **Love for God [is] best demonstrated and authenticated by loving one's neighbor.**
> **—Andy Stanley**

Session 4

BETWEEN SESSIONS

In each of these "Between Sessions" segments, you'll find an extended excerpt from Andy's book followed by questions for reflection.

THE EXCERPT

Jesus redefined *neighbor*.

For everybody.

Forever.

From this point forward, no one would have the latitude to limit the definition of *neighbor* to people like themselves. . . .

Jesus expanded *neighbor* beyond the boundaries of Judea and Galilee, beyond a single ethnicity. He broadened the definition beyond his first-century setting. And he did it with one perfectly timed and designed question. A question that continues to force even the most upright among us to examine our hearts and prejudices, our innate contempt for those who aren't like us. For more than two millennia, believers and skeptics alike have felt the weight of this parable and its inescapably disruptive closing question. . . .

Neighbor-love had no ethnic or geographical limits. Neighbor-love was evidence of God-love. It would be difficult to find a work-around or a loophole for this. If loving one's neighbor was the ultimate expression of one's love and devotion to God, the temple and everything associated with it suddenly became less important.

Perhaps unnecessary.

This was new indeed.

GIVE IT SOME THOUGHT

➡ In the passage above, Andy describes our tendency to stick to our kind as "innate contempt for those who aren't like us." What does this phrase mean to you?

➡ When have you personally experienced *innate contempt* for people who are unlike you? How did your reaction make you feel? Describe the situation in the space below.

➡ What is it about the human experience that drives *fear of the other*? What is it about walking with Jesus that puts that fear to rest?

In the parable of the Good Samaritan, we see not only the overcoming of fear of the other, but also an overcoming of practical obstacles that always must be scaled if we are to help another human being. Read Luke 10:25–37 and note which obstacles the Samaritan overcame.

➡️ **Which type of obstacle usually trips you up most when you're considering whether to extend yourself on behalf of another person?**

- The emotional investment, having to see—and really see—another's suffering

- The financial investment, having to give what I work so hard to obtain

- The investment of time, having to forego other important activities, to serve this one in need

- The investment of perseverance, having to stay in touch with someone in need over the long haul, having to check in again and again, having to stay the course

In the space below, put a few words to why you feel the sting of this investment.

➡️ **Take a moment to read Jesus' counsel to his disciples in Matthew 6:19–34. How might people who prioritize kingdom living experience fulfillment in earthly life?**

Caring for others can take on a thousand different forms. You might serve people in the community who have no food or shelter. You might tutor children who are preliterate. You might be intentional about learning more about people who look different, vote differently, or practice different lifestyles than you do.

➡ If you were to shift your focus from one of *vertical morality* to one of *horizontal morality*, where might you begin? Which of your "neighbors" comes to mind when you think of the needs of those around you? Spend a few moments brainstorming ideas in the space below before closing off your "Between Sessions" time.

REMINDER: To prepare for Session 5, be sure to read Chapters 15–20 in *Irresistible*.

SESSION 5

What Love Requires

The old covenant commands were part of the old covenant. . . . Jesus didn't issue his *new command* as an additional commandment to the existing list of commands. Jesus issued his new commandment as a *replacement* for everything in the existing list. Including the Big Ten.

Andy Stanley

BEFORE YOU BEGIN

A quick reminder before you dive in:

Session 5 covers material from six chapters in *Irresistible*:

- Chapter 15 :: A New Command

- Chapter 16 :: Paul and the Irresistible Ethic

- Chapter 17 :: It's Mutual

- Chapter 18 :: Don't Even Think about It

- Chapter 19 :: A Better Question

- Chapter 20 :: What Love Required of Me

FROM *IRRESISTIBLE* . . .

Before playing this session's video, have a group member read the following:

As the hinge between covenants, Jesus' mission was to lay the ground-work for the transition from old to new. Summarizing the entire Jewish law with two existing laws wasn't just genius, it was strategic. Just as the old covenant included laws for the nation to live by, so Jesus' new covenant would include instructions for his followers to live by as well. But his list wouldn't be engraved on stone tablets. It would be engraved in the hearts, minds, and consciences of his followers. The rules and regulations associated with Jesus' new covenant could easily be committed to memory. The reason being, they weren't a *they*. They were an *it*.

VIDEO NOTES

As you watch Session 5 of the video, feel free to take notes in the space below.

Jesus' new command

Love that's anchored in a person

Believing versus doing

Leveraging not power, but example

Less complicated, more demanding

An answer to "why" without an eye to the sky

DISCUSSION QUESTIONS

Cover as many of the following questions as time and group interest permit.

1. What did you think of this session's video segment? Compelling? Convicting? Either, neither, both?

2. Andy said, "Jesus wasn't commanding his followers to *feel* something. He was commanding them to *do* something." What do you make of this remark? Can you "do" love without first "feeling" love?

3. You could say that the big shift in Jesus' "new" commandment was from the perspective of selfishness to that of selflessness, from that of *self* to that of *Christ*. The Golden Rule, which summed up the Law, the old covenant way of life, stated, "So in everything, do to others what *you* would have them do to you," (Matthew 7:12, italics added). The "Platinum Rule," as Andy calls it, states, "Love each other as *I* have loved you," (John 15:12, italics added). Why was such a shift necessary for God to accomplish his redemptive plan?

4. Think back on your own spiritual journey. How would you put into words the love you've received from Christ? What shape has divine love taken in your mind and heart and life? Log your thoughts in the space below before sharing them with your group.

5. What difference do you think Jesus expects his love to make in and through your life?

WRAP IT UP

Remind participants of the "Between Sessions" material that follows, offer a closing thought or prayer based on the quote below, and then dismiss Session 5.

> Jesus' love *for* you, not his authority *over* you, is what he leverages to inspire you.
> —Andy Stanley

Session 5

BETWEEN SESSIONS

In each of these "Between Sessions" segments, you'll find an extended excerpt from Andy's book followed by questions for reflection.

THE EXCERPT

Jesus didn't tether his new command to the anchor all Jewish commands were traditionally tethered to: love for, fear of, dedication to God. Jesus tethered his new command to . . . this is big . . . to himself. Again, he inserted himself into an equation mere mortals have no business inserting themselves into.

Woven into all this subtlety was a not-so-subtle shift from vertical to horizontal. The eye-to-the-sky days were coming to an end. The litmus test for being a bona fide Jesus follower was not the ritualistic, day-of-the-week, festival-driven, don't-forget-your-goat worship of an invisible and somewhat distant God.

Following Jesus would not be about looking for ways to get closer to God who dwelled out there, up there, somewhere. Jesus followers would demonstrate their devotion to God by putting the person next to them in front of them. Jesus followers weren't expected to look up. They authenticated their devotion by looking around.

But the shift didn't stop there.

Conspicuously absent from Jesus' new-command instructions was an overt reference to his divine right to require such allegiance and obedience. In what is arguably his most future-defining set of instructions, Jesus refused to play the God card. Even in this final, if-you-forget-everything-else-I've-said-remember-this exchange, Jesus did not leverage his holiness, his personal righteousness, or even his divinely granted moral authority.

Jesus leveraged his example—how he loved.

GIVE IT SOME THOUGHT

➡ As you revisit Jesus' new command to love others as he has loved you, what emotions do you feel? Do you feel indicted? Encouraged? Affirmed for the approach to life you already take? Something else?

➡ If you were to more fully embrace this singular instruction from Jesus: "Love as I have loved you," what would you hope to experience more of in life?

➡ In the areas Andy cited in this session's video segment, what shifts do you think would occur were you to more faithfully prioritize love? Write your thoughts and hopes in the spaces below.

My intimate relationships

My work life

My parenting

How I interact with my friends

How I reach out to and respond to my neighbors

My relationships at church

How I steward my time

How I steward my money

My private life

The spiritual disciplines I practice

➡ Where do you stand to realize the *greatest growth* by making this practice of *Christ-fueled love* the governing ethic of your life? Note your thoughts below.

According to the apostle Paul, God's Spirit
will always nudge us in the direction of
kindness, goodness, gentleness, faithfulness,
and self-control. When in doubt, max
those out. That's what love requires.
—*Andy Stanley*

REMINDER: To prepare for Session 6, be sure to read the Introduction to Section 4 and Chapters 21–24 in *Irresistible*.

SESSION 6

A New Approach

If we're going to reach unchurched, under-churched, de-churched, and post-churched folks with the new covenant, new command message of Jesus in a culture that's trending post-Christian, we must rethink our *approach*.

Andy Stanley

BEFORE YOU BEGIN

A quick reminder before you dive in:

Session 6 covers material fom the Introduction to Section 4 and four chapters in *Irresistible*:

- Introduction to Section 4: A New Approach

- Chapter 21 :: Dorothy Was Right

- Chapter 22 :: Name Callers

- Chapter 23 :: First Things First

- Chapter 24 :: The Bible Says

FROM *IRRESISTIBLE* . . .

Before playing this session's video, have a group member read the following:

If we're going to reach unchurched, under-churched, de-churched, and post-churched folks with the new covenant, new command message of Jesus in a culture that's trending post-Christian, we must rethink our *approach*. The right message with the wrong approach yields the wrong results. This is why parents obsess over how to *approach* their kids on certain topics. They know what needs to be communicated. But the wrong approach has the potential to send an important conversation in the wrong direction.

But there's another reason parents obsess over their approach.

They care.

When you care about someone, you're never content to simply make your point. When you care about someone, your goal is to make a difference. So you think long and hard about your approach.

VIDEO NOTES

As you watch Session 6 of the video, feel free to take notes in the spaces below.

The beauty of de-conversion stories

Jesus has never been the stumbling block.

Why the first disciples stuck around

Which is the cart, which is the horse?

How to re-become irresistible

Exceptional, exception-al Katherine

DISCUSSION QUESTIONS

Cover as many of the following questions as time and group interest permit.

1. How did this video segment sit with you? What part of it stuck with you most, and why?

2. Andy notes that people don't generally leave the church or the faith because of Jesus and that Jesus has never been the stumbling block. For the people you know who have fallen away from church or faith or the things of God, what caused them to lose interest?

3. What do you think your response would be to those who left if they were to come to you for input?

4. In terms of how to reach out to those who have left, Andy wrote the following:

> In our post-Christian culture, making better churches isn't the answer. The answer is a return to the resurrection-centered, new covenant, love-one-another version of our faith ... The version of faith that got this thing kicked off to begin with. Unchurched people may not be interested in church, but they certainly want to be *one-anothered*. Especially when things aren't going well. Post-Christians could not care less about my new sermon series. But they're still interested in matters of faith and spirituality ....
>
> Most post-Christians still have a crush on Jesus.

What would you hope this "one-anothering" would include if you were on the receiving end?

5. In *Irresistible*, Andy made a series of provocative claims regarding what's possible when people "outside the faith" are treated not with disdain but with dignity. He wrote:

> It's remarkable what happens when people don't feel like they have to choose between science and Christianity. It's remarkable what happens when Jewish folks are given the option to follow Jesus' teaching without feeling pressured to embrace him as Messiah. It's remarkable what happens when a high school student realizes the creation story is not the make or break for her faith. It's remarkable what happens when you give skeptics the benefit of the doubt . . . .

> It's remarkable what happens when you allow people to discover they are sinners rather than accusing them of it. It's remarkable what happens when thoughtful Christians, who for years harbored secret doubts and questions, discover that the foundation of their faith is not an inerrant text or non-contradicting Gospels. It's remarkable what happens when college freshmen discover that the violence and unsubstantiated historical references in the Old Testament don't undermine the message of Jesus. It's remarkable what happens when a biology major discovers his Christian faith doesn't teeter on the brink of irrelevance based on how long it took the universe to form.

> It's remarkable what happens when thoughtful, educated, skeptical men and women are invited to embrace the message of Jesus without having to believe a man put two of every kind of animal on a boat after which God flooded the world and killed everybody but that man and his family.

Any of these hit home for you? What about for friends and family members you love? Which of the above statements make you want to stand up and cheer? Anything you'd add to this list?

- _____

- _____

On the other side of the equation, which of the items above strike a note of fear in your heart? Any of them elicit strong feelings of insecurity or clinginess? ("What? Now we don't believe in the great flood?") Any of them make you wonder if, based on the abandoning of that *one key issue*, your faith simply could not stand?

6. As a group, consider these three questions:

   a. If nothing about the version of Christianity we espouse today were to change, how would you describe the type of faith that would be passed to our children and their children?

   b. How does that hypothetical reality you just described compare with your *hopes and dreams* for the faith we pass down?

   c. What do you think reclaiming our *irresistibility* will require of us collectively? What might it require of you?

WRAP IT UP

Remind participants of the "Between Sessions" material that follows, offer a closing thought or prayer based on the quote below, and then dismiss Session 6.

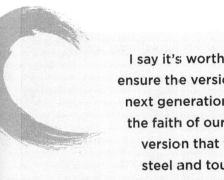

I say it's worth any change necessary to
ensure the version of faith passed on to the
next generation is the enduring version—
the faith of our first-century fathers. The
version that was harder than Roman
steel and tougher than Roman nails.
—*Andy Stanley*

Session 6

BETWEEN SESSIONS

In each of these "Between Sessions" segments, you'll find an extended excerpt from Andy's book followed by questions for reflection.

THE EXCERPT

Every generation of Christians is required to engage their generation with the new covenant claims of Jesus. [The apostle] Peter said it best.

> But in your hearts revere Christ as Lord. Always be prepared to give an answer to everyone who asks you to give the reason for the hope that you have.

The word *answer* in our English Bibles comes from the Greek term *apologia*, from which we get our English words *apology* and *apologetics*. So as not to miss the important connection between the two ideas in Peter's statement, I'll mix 'em up a bit.

> Always be prepared to provide an explanation to everyone who asks you to explain why you've chosen to put your hope in Christ and make him your Lord.

Every generation of believers must be prepared to defend their decision to follow Jesus. But Peter's exhortation implies something else. Something we dare not miss. Every generation of believers must be prepared to explain their decision to follow Jesus *in* their generation *to* their generation out of concern *for* their generation. Peter knew that. He wanted to make sure his original audience knew it as well. So he adds:

> But do this with gentleness and respect, keeping a clear conscience, so that those who speak maliciously against your good behavior in Christ may be ashamed of their slander.

So there it is.

Our new covenant marching orders.

We're to be prepared with a verbal explanation for why we've chosen to follow Jesus. And while we make our reasons known, we're to live in such a way that our behavior underscores rather than undermines our message. There was a time when *the Bible says* was reason enough. And while it may still be reason enough for you, it's no reason at all for a significant percentage of the population.

GIVE IT SOME THOUGHT

➡ In reading the above excerpt, is the prevailing emotion you experience more akin to indictment and regret or to encouragement and energy to keep moving ahead? Something else? Note your thoughts before moving on.

➡ Andy's first assertion centers on the idea of engaging our generation with the new covenant claims of Jesus. What do you think such engagement looks like? What might it include?

➡ This "engagement" has much to do with our individual stories of redemption and restoration, our stories of personally interacting with the grace and love of Christ. Which begs a question: *What is your story?*

If it's been awhile since you thought through the change Jesus has facilitated in your life, then take this opportunity to complete the prompts below.

Before I met Jesus, I would say I was . . .

My biggest priorities/goals during that time of my life were . . .

I was willing to entertain a spiritual dimension to my life because . . .

I discovered the person of Jesus through . . .

What I noticed about Christianity was . . .

The qualms I brought with me as I gave my life to Jesus were . . .

I addressed those doubts, fears, and insecurities by . . .

The most significant gain I experienced when first following Christ was . . .

Since then, I'd characterize my faith journey as being one of . . .

➡ Look back at your completed prompts. If you were to sum up your spiritual journey thus far, what words would you use?

- Jesus helped me make the shift from being fearful to becoming confident.

- Jesus helped me make the shift from being a spendthrift to becoming a steward.

- Jesus helped me make the shift from being selfish to becoming committed to helping others.

- Jesus helped me make the shift from being unfaithful to becoming faithful.

- Jesus helped me make the shift from being cynical to becoming hopeful.

- Jesus helped me make the shift from being antagonistic to becoming collaborative.

- Jesus helped me make the shift from being legalistic to becoming free.

➡ Now, it's your turn. What before-and-after difference has Jesus made for you?

"Jesus has helped me make the shift from being _____ to becoming _____."

In the passage we looked at earlier, the apostle Peter makes a remarkable assumption. Not only does he encourage us to have a ready explanation for why we follow Jesus, but also he suggests that people will ask us for that explanation. Let's revisit the original text. It reads: "In your hearts revere Christ as Lord. Always be prepared to give an answer to everyone who asks you to give the reason for the hope that you have" (1 Peter 3:15).

Which begs another question: *When's the last time someone asked?*

➡ When was the last time someone asked about your patience in a chaotic scene?

➡ When was the last time someone asked about your gentleness when someone was rude?

➡ When was the last time someone asked about your goodness in an evil world?

➡ When was the last time someone asked about your hopefulness when all seemed lost?

➡ What kinds of choices create a life that people ask about? What prompts people to spot Jesus in *you*? Note your thoughts below.

1. _____

2. _____

3. _____

4. _____

5. _____

6. _____

And finally, there's the issue of *how.*

How do we share our stories?

How do we choose to live life?

Again, from the apostle Peter: "But do this with gentleness and respect keeping a clear conscience, so that those who speak maliciously against your good behavior in Christ may be ashamed of their slander" (1 Peter 3:15–16).

Every generation of believers must be
prepared to explain their decision to follow
Jesus *in* their generation *to* their generation
out of concern *for* their generation.
—*Andy Stanley*

This love I've received from Jesus . . .

What might it require of me?

➡ What might *gentleness* be asking of you today?

➡ How might *respectfulness* show itself strong?

Follow Video Study

Andy Stanley

Lots of people think Christianity is all about doing what Jesus says. But what if doing what Jesus says isn't what Jesus says to do at all? Jesus' invitation is an invitation to relationship, and it begins with a simple request: follow me.

Religion says "Change and you can join us." Jesus says, "Join us and you will change." There's a huge difference. Jesus doesn't expect people to be perfect. He just wants them to follow him. Being a sinner doesn't disqualify anyone. Being an unbeliever doesn't disqualify anyone. In fact, following almost always begins with a sinner and unbeliever taking one small step.

In this eight-session video-based Bible study (participant's guide sold separately), Andy Stanley takes small groups on a journey through the Gospels as he traces Jesus' teaching on what it means to follow.

Sessions include:

1. Jesus Says
2. Next Steps
3. Fearless
4. Follow Wear
5. The Fine Print
6. What I Want to Want
7. Leading Great
8. Unfollow

Available in stores and online!

Christian Video Study

It's Not What You Think

Andy Stanley

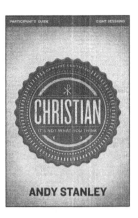

According to Andy Stanley, the words used to describe Christians today often bear no resemblance to what Jesus wanted his followers to be known for.

In this eight-session video study (participant's guide sold separately), you'll learn:

- What one word should be descriptive of every Christian
- How Jesus' followers should treat those who are outside the faith
- Why people love Jesus but can't stand his followers

Sessions include:

1. Brand Recognition
2. Quitters
3. Insiders, Outsiders
4. Showing Up
5. When Gracie Met Truthy
6. Angry Birds
7. Loopholes
8. Working It Out

Guardrails DVD Study

Avoiding Regret in Your Life

Andy Stanley

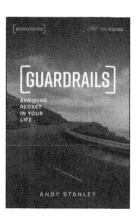

[Guardrails: a system designed to keep vehicles from straying into dangerous or off-limit areas.]

They're everywhere, but they don't really get much attention . . . until somebody hits one. And then, more often than not, it is a lifesaver.

Ever wonder what it would be like to have guardrails in other areas of your life—areas where culture baits you to the edge of disaster and then chastises you when you step across the line?

Your friendships. Your finances. Your marriage. Maybe your greatest regret could have been avoided if you had established guardrails.

In this six-session video based study (participant's guide sold separately), Andy Stanley challenges us to stop flirting with disaster and establish some personal guardrails.

Session titles:

1. Direct and Protect
2. Why Can't We Be Friends
3. Flee Baby Flee!
4. Me and the Mrs.
5. The Consumption Assumption
6. Once and For All